GLOBAL ISSUES BIBLE STUDIES

Series editors: Stephen Hayner & Gordon Aeschliman

*S*ANCTITY OF *L*IFE

E. Dawn Swaby-Ellis

6 Studies
for individuals
or groups

INTERVARSITY PRESS
DOWNERS GROVE, ILLINOIS 60515

InterVarsity Press is the book-publishing division of InterVarsity Christian Fellowship, a student movement active on campus at hundreds of universities, colleges and schools of nursing in the United States of America, and a member movement of the International Fellowship of Evangelical Students. For information about local and regional activities, write Public Relations Dept., InterVarsity Christian Fellowship, 6400 Schroeder Rd., P.O. Box 7895, Madison, WI 53707-7895.

All Scripture quotations, unless otherwise indicated, are from the Holy Bible, New International Version. Copyright © 1973, 1978, International Bible Society. Used by permission of Zondervan Bible Publishers.

Cover illustration: TransLight

ISBN 0-8308-4911-4

Printed in the United States of America

| 12 | 11 | 10 | 9 | 8 | 7 | 6 | 5 | 4 | 3 | 2 | 1 |
| 99 | 98 | 97 | 96 | 95 | 94 | 93 | 92 | 91 | 90 | | |

Contents

Welcome to Global Issues Bible Studies ——— 5

Introducing Sanctity of Life ——— 10

1/What Is Life? ——— 21

2/Dignity of Life ——— 25

3/Abortion ——— 28

4/War ——— 33

5/Capital Punishment ——— 37

6/A Biblical View of Life ——— 41

Suggestions for Leaders ——— 45

Resources ——— 48

Because humankind is made in the image of God, every person, regardless of race, religion, color, culture, class, sex or age, has an intrinsic dignity because of which he or she should be respected and served, not exploited. Here too we express penitence both for our neglect and for having sometimes regarded evangelism and social concern as mutually exclusive.

Although reconciliation with people is not reconciliation with God, nor is social action evangelism, nor is political liberation salvation, nevertheless we affirm that evangelism and sociopolitical involvement are both part of our Christian duty. For both are necessary expressions of our doctrines of God and humankind, our love for our neighbor and our obedience to Jesus Christ.

The message of salvation implies also a message of judgment upon every form of alienation, oppression and discrimination, and we should not be afraid to denounce evil and injustice wherever they exist.

—Lausanne Covenant, Article Five.

Welcome to Global Issues Bible Studies

With all the rapid and dramatic changes happening in our world today, it's easy to be overwhelmed and simply withdraw. But it need not be so for Christians! God has not only given us the mandate to love the world, he has given us the Holy Spirit and the community of fellowship to guide us and equip us in the ministry of love.

Ministering in the world can be threatening: It requires change in both our lifestyle and our thinking. We end up discovering that we need to cling closer to Jesus than ever before—and that becomes the great personal benefit of change. God's love for the world is the same deep love he has for you and me.

This study series is designed to help us understand what is going on in *the world*. Then it takes us to *the Word* to help us be faithful in our compassionate response. The series is firmly rooted in the evangelical tradition which calls for a personal saving relationship with Jesus Christ and a public lifestyle of discipleship that demonstrates the Word has truly come alive in us.

At the front of the guide is an excerpt from the Lausanne Covenant which we have found particularly helpful. We have developed
this series in keeping with the spirit of the covenant, especially sections four and five. You may wish to refer to the Lausanne Covenant
for further guidance as you form your own theology of evangelism
and social concern.

In the words of the covenant's authors we place this challenge
before you: "The salvation we claim should be transforming us in the
totality of our personal and social responsibilities. Faith without
works is dead."

Getting the Most from Global Issues Bible Studies
Global Issues Bible Studies are designed to be an exciting and chal-
lenging way to help us seek God's will for all of the world as it is
found in Scripture. As we learn more about the world, we will learn
more about ourselves as well.

How They Are Designed
Global Issues Bible Studies have a number of distinctive features.
First, each guide has an introduction from the author which will help
orient us to the subject at hand and the significant questions which
the studies will deal with.

Second, the Bible study portion is inductive rather than deductive.
In other words, the author will lead us to discover what the Bible says
about a particular topic through a series of questions rather than
simply telling us what he or she believes. Therefore, the studies are
thought-provoking. They help us to think about the meaning of the
passage so that we can truly understand what the biblical writer
intended to say.

Third, the studies are personal. Global Issues Bible Studies are not
just theoretical studies to be considered in private or discussed in a
group. These studies will motivate us to action. They will expose us
to the promises, assurances, exhortations and challenges of God's

Word. Through the study of Scripture, we will renew our minds so that we can be transformed by the Spirit of God.

Fourth, the guides include resource sections that will help you to act on the challenges Scripture has presented you with.

Fifth, these studies are versatile. They are designed for student, mission, neighborhood and/or church groups. They are also effective for individual study.

How They Are Put Together

Global Issues Bible Studies also have a distinctive format. Each study need take no more than forty-five minutes in a group setting or thirty minutes in personal study—unless you choose to take more time.

Each guide has six studies. If the guides are used in pairs, they can be used within a quarter system in a church and fit well in a semester or trimester system on a college campus.

The guides have a workbook format with space for writing responses to each question. This is ideal for personal study and allows group members to prepare in advance for the discussion. In addition the last question in each study offers suggestions and opportunity for personal response.

At the end of the guides are some notes for leaders. They describe how to lead a group discussion, give helpful tips on group dynamics and suggest ways to deal with problems which may arise during the discussion. With such helps, someone with little or no experience can lead an effective study.

Suggestions for Individual Study

1. As you begin the study, pray that God will help you understand and apply the passages to your life. Pray that he will show you what kinds of action he would have you take as a result of your time of study.

2. In your first session take time to read the introduction to the entire guide. This will orient you to the subject at hand and the author's goals for the studies.

3. Read the short introduction to the study.

4. Read and reread the suggested Bible passages to familiarize yourself with them.

5. A good modern translation of the Bible, rather than the King James Version or a paraphrase, will give you the most help. The New International Version, the New American Standard Bible and the Revised Standard Version are all recommended. The questions in this guide are based on the New International Version.

6. Use the space provided to respond to the questions. This will help you express your understanding of the passage clearly.

7. Look up the passages listed under *For Further Study* at the end of each study. This will help you to better understand the principles outlined in the main passages and give you an idea of how these themes are found throughout Scripture.

8. It might be good to have a Bible dictionary handy. Use it to look up any unfamiliar words, names or places.

9. Take time with the final question in each study to commit yourself to action and/or a change in attitude.

Suggestions for Group Study

1. Come to the study prepared. Follow the suggestions for individual study mentioned above. You will find that careful preparation will greatly enrich your time spent in group discussion.

2. Be willing to participate in the discussion. The leader of your group will not be lecturing. Instead, he or she will be encouraging the members of the group to discuss what they have learned. The leader will be asking the questions that are found in this guide.

3. Stick to the topic being discussed. Your answers should be based on the verses which are the focus of the discussion and not on outside authorities such as commentaries or speakers.

4. Be sensitive to the other members of the group. Listen attentively when they describe what they have learned. You may be surprised by their insights! When possible, link what you say to the comments of others. Also, be affirming whenever you can. This will encourage

some of the more hesitant members of the group to participate.

5. Be careful not to dominate the discussion. We are sometimes so eager to express our thoughts that we leave too little opportunity for others to respond. By all means participate! But allow others to also.

6. Expect God to teach you through the passage being discussed and through the other members of the group. Pray that you will have an enjoyable and profitable time together, but also that as a result of the study, you will find ways that you can take action individually and/or as a group.

7. If you are the discussion leader, you will find additional suggestions at the back of the guide.

God bless you in your adventure of love.

Steve Hayner
Gordon Aeschliman

Introducing Sanctity of Life

As a young physician, I was confronted with two women requesting abortions. One was a mother of five children, the last three of whom had been admitted to the hospital suffering from severe malnutrition. This mother's physical resources had not improved, and she lived in a country where public assistance programs were very limited. The second was a mother requesting an abortion on her fifteen-year-old daughter, who had been the victim of rape.

Rationally, it seemed quite clear that neither of these infants would enjoy a good quality of life. The first mother could not cope with the children she already had. How would the inevitable malnutrition affect the developing brain of her fetus? What suffering would result? What real hope was there of breaking this cycle of poverty and continuous reproduction? An abortion and tubal ligation seemed to be the obvious solution.

The second mother was an innocent schoolgirl, who was doing well scholastically and had a bright future ahead of her. She was horrified at the "thing" growing in her. What chance could the infant possibly have of being loved and nurtured? Given the cruelty of its conception, what hope could it have for health and happiness?

Some years later, while attending a conference of Christian health professionals in England, I was convicted about my actions. I was speaking to a missionary recently returned from Africa. As I told her about my experiences with the two mothers and how I felt sure that rational thought processes had to be applied to the abortion debate, she listened attentively—her eyes were kind. She gave me a small tract. It did not offer me new information. It related the sequential steps in fetal development from the fetus's point of view: "Today, I have fingers. I can hear my mother's heartbeat. I can move around. I am growing. I am eleven inches long. . . ." Then, with shocking abruptness: "Today, my mother killed me."

As I continued to read the little tract, my mind raced to the two mothers. "Thou shalt not kill," says one of the Ten Commandments. "God is the giver of life; he knows us from our mother's womb," according to the psalmist.

"But," I asked the missionary, "what about the likelihood of the fifth child's also becoming malnourished? What of the rejection the child of rape would be likely to face?"

My friend responded gently: "You do not know the future. You are responsible only to be obedient to what you know to be the will of God."

Years later, I was again faced with a mother who felt that she did not have the resources to bring another child into the world. She already had two children and was estranged from their father, with no possibility of employment. I told her that the life within her was precious to God, that she should go home and read Psalm 139 and think about what it said. I prayed with her that God would give her the resources and love for the child, and that her children's father would accept responsibility for them.

I had the privilege of re-establishing contact with that family during a recent trip to Jamaica, ten years after our first meeting. I spoke to the father, who told me that they were married. They had had not only the child I spoke of, but also another. The father was doing very well in a recording business, and they had moved into their own house.

I tell these stories because, although the circumstances of the various women were not the same, my action on the second occasion was governed by obedience to God and his Word. My action on the first was governed by reasoned argument based on visible life-circumstances and experience. The educated person will always tend to trust the reasoned argument. The mind is one of our greatest God-given assets; yet we are called to live the three-dimensional life of body, mind and spirit. This life in obedience to God's Word demands that we sometimes walk out in pure faith, in direct antithesis of apparent reason and logic, trusting that God knows what he is doing and that his way is always right.

The Struggle to Define Life

In the 1990s, as in ancient times, we still seek the answers to the questions What is life? and Where does life come from?

In a general sense, among most people and nations in the world, life is valued, and there are laws forbidding the taking of life. Nevertheless, we are bombarded daily with complex situations that challenge our understanding of the commandment "Thou shalt not kill." As Christians, we seek biblical answers to questions about abortion, capital punishment, euthanasia and the use of nuclear weapons. Is there a Christian view of life that would help us to address these issues?

We would all agree with the definition that life is that quality that distinguishes a vital and functional being from a dead body.[1] In other words, that which is not dead is alive. Scientists tend to define life according to their own specializations, but are not able to agree on one definition: "Despite the enormous fund of information that each of these biological specialties has provided, it is a remarkable fact that no general agreement exists on what it is that is being studied. There is no generally accepted definition of life."[2]

We now have the capability to fertilize an ovum outside of the uterus, in a test tube. We have a growing understanding of some of the 100,000 genes that make up the human genome, and the capacity to replace defective genes with normal ones. Genetic engineering in humans is the subject of increasing public debate and ethical scrutiny, forcing us to consider what is at the root of our concern for the manipulation of human life as opposed to plant life.

The publicity around the abortion debate—filled as it is with angry groups bearing placards and shouting at one another across police barricades—and the endless arguing of rights (the right of a woman versus the right of the state) may have dulled our minds to the essential question: Is this a question of life versus death?

If fetal life is life, what is the value of that life?

In addition we must ask questions about warfare and whether or not it is appropriate in light of how we view life. What is the basis for a decision to fight and kill a people of a different race or culture from ourselves? What value are we placing on their lives? What value are we placing on the lives of those who are in our own armies?

As the Iron Curtain comes tumbling down, as Poland, Hungary, Romania, Czechoslovakia and Bulgaria embrace democracy as a way of life, who is our enemy? The United States invaded South Vietnam to prevent a communist takeover; now, a few decades later, we are establishing close ties with the Soviet Union and beginning trade partnerships with the Eastern Bloc. Does this mean that the blood shed in Vietnam was shed in vain? Or could the fledgling Eastern Bloc democracies be the firstfruits of that sacrifice? These are all difficult questions, thought-provoking questions, with no easy answers.

Apart from the fact that well-respected encyclopedias cannot easily define life, let alone the value or purpose of life, there is little consensus on life's origins. Did life arise spontaneously—organic from inorganic matter? Did it then slowly progress from lower to higher forms. Did life appear on earth in response to some supernatural series of events, or was it specially and intentionally created?

The first chapter of the Bible begins: "In the beginning God created the heavens and the earth. Now the earth was formless and empty, darkness was over the surface of the deep, and the Spirit of God was hovering over the waters" (Gen 1:1-2). The passage that follows elaborates on the sequence of the creation of light (signifying the day) and darkness (signifying the night), the creation of sky, land and sea, and then the production of plant life from the land. After the placing of the sun, moon and stars, the waters became inhabited with living creatures, birds flew in the sky, and the land was occupied by all kinds of living creatures, including animals.

The final act of creation was the fashioning of human beings, male and female, in the image and likeness of God. They were given authority over all other living creatures and naming rights. They were also to work the land and take care of it. The description of the creation of humans is further elaborated in Genesis 2: "The LORD God formed the man from the dust of the ground and breathed into his nostrils the breath of life, and the man became a living being" (v. 7).

Whether this account in Genesis is allegorical or literal, whether it argues for or against the Darwinian theory of evolution and natural selection, it is clear on three points, which are essential to the Christian view of life:

1. God is the Author and Creator of all life.
2. Human beings are the high point of creation, made in the image of God.
3. Humans are in charge of the rest of creation and accountable to God for the rest of life on the planet.

Whose idea was it that life should exist? The biblical answer is that life was God's idea. It is he who gives life to all creatures.

An important distinction must now be made between humankind and all other forms of life. Other animals and plants carry out the daily physiological and biochemical functions of life just as human beings do, but the human species is singular in the capacity for reason, the possession of conscience, the ability to reflect and introspect, the desire to seek fellowship with a higher being, and the drive to fulfill lofty aspirations, performing superhuman or transcendent feats. This is René Descartes's "thinking individual," the indwelling personality much studied by psychologists and philosophers, the one made in the image of God.

What has the Bible to say about human life?

The Greek words used for "life" in the Bible do not translate easily into English, but they are helpful for understanding the teaching of both Old and New Testaments. The word for mere existence, *bios,* is used in reference to unborn human life, life in infancy, life dominated by sensate satisfactions— biological, physical life. It is employed by Jesus when speaking of the widow's mite—"all she had to live on" (Mk 12:44)—and describing the prodigal son's style of living (Lk 15:13). *Psychē* has a broader meaning, encompassing the life of the soul, the ego, the mind: "Greater love has no one than this, that he lay down his psuche for his friends" (Jn 15:13). *Psychē* constitutes life with more potential than *bios,* and is the life that the majority of human beings live at any given moment. *Zōē* is the word used predominantly in John's Gospel, connoting life in the Spirit, or eternal life: "I have come that they may have life, and have it to the full" (Jn 10:10), and "In him was life, and that life was the light of men" (Jn 1:4).

In his excellent book *Human Life,* J. Robert Nelson explains that these three concepts of life are not to be viewed separately but as three dimensions of one life.[3] Thus, the Christian view of humankind acknowledges the biological characteristics that make *Homo sapiens* part of the mammalian family, the higher mental functions that enable humans to reason and be in charge of the rest of creation, and the spiritual capacity to experience life in Jesus Christ, once they have been born again by the power of the Spirit.

Questions of Meaning

What then is the purpose and meaning of our lives?

We are told by the writer of Genesis that God created men and women for fellowship with himself, to care for his creation, to be fruitful and replenish the earth with progeny, and to be obedient to God's commands.

As the giver of life, God holds us accountable for how we live our lives. We are his possession, his purchased possession—bought with a price (1 Cor 6:20; 7:23). Every hair on our heads is numbered by God (Mt 10:30). We are known by him before we are conceived (Jer 1:5) and throughout our fetal development (Ps 139:13).

In addition to having a unique genetic makeup, each of us has a particular calling and gifts (1 Cor 12:7-11; 1 Pet 4:10), given to us by God for use in edifying the body of believers and, as in the parable of the talents, for bearing fruit for him. Our stewardship of our gifts will be evaluated by him on the day of accounting (Lk 19:11-27; Mt 25:14-28).

Our lives with God are in relationship to him. As Christians, we believe that this relationship was broken by sin and then re-established by the supreme sacrificial act of his Son, Jesus, who died on the cross for our sin so that the original fellowship of human beings with God could be restored. One way that we get to know God is through his Word, for that is one of his principal means of self-revelation.

We are responsible before God as individuals but also as members of communities, for he commands us not only to love him with all our hearts, souls, minds and strength but also to love our neighbors as ourselves. We are accountable to each other, then, to love one another and to bear one another's burdens (Gal 6:2). Resisting the individualism that is rampant in our culture, we are to live and think as a body of believers, the strong supporting the weak, the rich supporting the poor, the healthy supporting the sick. Such are the relationships to which we are called—in single life, in marriage, within the body of the church, and within the world.

The Christian's purpose for living is also to glorify Christ by lifting him up in the world so that he may draw people to himself. We do this by the witness of our daily lives, by our personal and corporate testimony, by using every opportunity presented to tell others of the hope that is in us, the hope of eternal life.

As a pediatrician, I have been in many delivery rooms and experienced the incredible joy and sense of worshipful awe that accompanies the birth of a child into the world. The words of an Indian poet always seem so apt: "Each child comes with the message that God is not yet discouraged with man."

Yet there is also that profound moment at a Christian funeral when we sing, through our tears: "It is well, it is well with my soul." We sing because we know that our loved one has gone on to the place where there shall be no more suffering, for "God himself will be with them and be their God. He will wipe every tear from their eyes" (Rev 21:3-4). Every Christian lives with this hope. Here on earth we begin to experience eternal life as we grow in knowledge of God and in the abundance of his life.

A Precious Gift

What value does the Christian place on life?

We have seen that life is a gift of God, with a defined meaning and purpose. The Bible tells us that we are precious to God, who counts every hair on our head and lists our tears on his scroll (Ps 56:8). We have seen that we live in three dimensions: the essential physical, mechanistic life that we share with other animals, the life of aspiration and reason that we share with other humans, and life in the Spirit, which is also the life to come.

The value of our lives involves our readiness to give it away, to lay it down, to lose it that we may find it (Mt 16:25). We are told in Scripture not to worry about it (Mt 6:25), not to try to save it, and not to fear him who can destroy the earthly part of it (Mt 10:28; Lk 12:5). Writing to the Philippian church, Paul gives a stirring description of how he understands the value of his life and all his worldly achievements in the light of his all-encompassing goal: "I consider everything a loss compared to the surpassing greatness of knowing Christ Jesus my Lord, for whose sake I have lost all things" (Phil 3:8).

Facing the Questions

Is there then a Christian way of life?

Church history tells us that even among Christians consensus on any pressing question is seldom achieved. Thus, it is not surprising that there are Christians on both sides of the abortion debate, Christians who favor the death penalty and those who abhor capital punishment, and Christians who marshal biblical justification for their willingness to take up arms and others who support their commitment to nonviolent protest with reference to Scripture.

Such diversity of opinions should not deter us from our individual search for solutions, nor should it lead us to minimize the importance of clearly defining our own position on these issues. To live as salt and light in the world, we must be noticeably different from the non-Christians who surround us. Even as food is enhanced by salt, our presence at a discussion on abortion, a senate debate on a new nuclear missile program, or a neighborhood meeting on crime prevention should make a difference.

The world needs Christ and the life that he brings. We are simply his humble representatives in the world, but he has promised to live through us if we let him. We must first believe in him and then, like Paul, be prepared to lose all that we may find him. It is in this spirit of reckless abandonment of all to Christ that we begin to experience *zōē,* the abundant life that he came to give.

At this point we begin to have the mind of Christ and can have something of his perspective on the issues of life and death that so perplex our world. It is precisely because we as Christians are at different points of the journey, with various emphases on one or another aspect of the three-dimensional life, that we end up with different solutions to the same problem. Add to that our varied life experiences and cultural biases, and the challenges to unity of opinion become quite obvious.

I believe that the Christian who would be true to his or her God has no choice but to enter the contemporary debate on burning issues such as abortion, nuclear war and mercy killing. Many of us will face the decision of whether to disconnect a loved one from a life-support machine. All of us in the work force will pay taxes which are used not only to provide housing for the poor but also to make missiles. There will come a time when scarce resources will force us to make hard choices about how our money is spent.

At those times of decision-making, we need a strong, biblically based code of conduct. We need a Christian ethic that expresses the value we place on life, as seen from the perspective of the One who is the Way, the Truth and the Life. His mission involved a concern for the poor, the oppressed, the prisoners, the brokenhearted. His kingdom is not of this world, and his concerns went far beyond the material pleasures of this life. He is full of compassion for sinners, for little children, for adulterers and for those who are sick.

He espoused a new philosophy. "Love your enemies," he said. Abandon retributive justice. Do good to those who would use you and persecute you; pray that God would forgive you for your wrongdoings as you forgive those who may have wronged you.

I am grateful for his promise of forgiveness. My own position on abortion changed completely when I took a good look at what the Bible has to say about life. Yet the struggle continues. I still must be concerned about the fate of the unwanted child, the lack of role models for our youth in inner cities, the dearth of foster homes or adoptive homes for abused children, the relatively scarce resources available for rehabilitation of drug addicts and juvenile offenders. These are all concerns for life.

To be authentically Christlike, we must be committed to peacemaking, advocating resolution of conflict by negotiation and arbitration, by nonviolent methods of protest rather than war. We must support deceleration of the arms race and more investment in the human race.

We must show respect for all human life, regardless of color, race or creed, for Christ came that all might be saved, that all barriers between one person and another might be broken down. Thus the sufferings of people in South Africa, Nicaragua and Lebanon are of equal concern to us. It is when we achieve an authentic witness of deep love for each life—a love only Jesus can give—that we are able to live his life in the world .

Above all, we have to live with the tension of not having all the final answers. In 1 Corinthians Paul puts it this way: "Now we see but a poor reflection as in a mirror; then we shall see face to face. Now I know in part; then I shall know fully, even as I am fully known" (1 Cor 13:12).

Martin Luther expresses this tension well:
This life therefore is not righteousness,
    but growth in righteousness,
Not health, but healing,
Not being, but becoming,
Not rest, but exercise.
We are not yet what we shall be, but
We are growing toward it.
This process is not yet finished,
But is going on.
This is not the end,
But it is the road.
All does not yet gleam in glory
But all is being purified.

"We are not yet what we shall be, but we are growing toward it" is a comforting and enabling reality as we approach a biblical study of life.

---

[1] *Webster's New Collegiate Dictionary* (1979), p. 658.
[2] *Encyclopaedia Britannica Macropaedia* (1978), p. 893.
[3] *Human Life* (Philadelphia: Fortress Press, 1984).

Study 1

What Is Life?

To a world that has not yet succeeded in defining life, there comes a man with a startling claim: "In him was life, and that life was the light of men. The light shines in the darkness, but the darkness has not understood it."

To understand who the writer of John's Gospel is talking about, and to gain a biblical perspective on life, we will start at the beginning—with the story of creation.

1. Have you experienced the abundant life that Jesus offers? Describe it.

Read John 1:1-14.

2. Who do these verses tell you was present in the beginning (vv. 1-2)?

Jesus Christ

Who created all things (vv. 3-4)?

Christ/God - one & the same

3. What is the meaning of life as it is described in verse 4?

to give light to all mankind — leading to eternal life

4. Who is the light described in verses 6-14?

Jesus Christ is the true Light

5. What was the mission of that light (vv. 12-14)?

to save mankind - spiritual rebirth

6. These verses set up a choice between life and death. What is the

choice described in verse 12?

to accept & receive him

Humanity's sinfulness causes God to bring a great flood upon the earth. God tells Noah to build an ark and saves Noah and his family. Read the promise God made to Moses following the flood in Genesis 9:1-7.

7. What instructions does God give in verses 2-3?

Gives man command over wild animals, birds and fish

8. What is the purpose of the instructions regarding "lifeblood" (vv. 4-5)?

9. What does verse 6 tell us about God's view of the sanctity of human life?

Read Matthew 6:25-34.

10. Over the past week, what aspects of your life have been of greatest concern to you?

11. Contrast the abundant life in Christ you described with the life in verses 25-27, with its concerns for food and clothing.

12. What understanding can you gain from verses 28-34 about Jesus' concern for meeting the physical as well as spiritual needs of our lives?

13. *Response:* Pray for a deeper understanding of the real meaning and purpose of your life in Christ.

For Further Study: Read Genesis 1 and Psalm 8 for further accounts of creation. Read John 3:16-18 for more on the choice between life and death. The Old Testament view of life is illustrated in Deuteronomy 30:11-20, when he sets before them the choice between life and death.

Dignity of Life

"What's the meaning? What's the meaning of life?"—Soul-II-Soul, 1990

This refrain from an Afro-British rhythm and blues group who call themselves *funky dreads* reflects humankind's quest for an understanding of our existence. One of the important aspects of this quest is the value question.

What is the value of life? In order to find life's value, we must look for the source of value. The value of life lies not so much in the worth of its material substance (minerals, proteins, chemicals) as in its relation to the intelligence that created it and the significance the Creator assigns to it. The value of human life is spiritual. It derives from the position given to human beings by the Creator in relation to all other created things, animate or inanimate.

1. What kinds of people does our society devalue? Give examples.

Read Genesis 1:26-31.
2. What is significant about the origin of life according to Genesis 1:26-31?

3. What does being created in the image of God (v. 27) tell us about a proper regard for human life?

Cain presented a careless, unloving offering to God, while his brother, Abel, offered his best. God rejected Cain's offering and accepted Abel's. Read Genesis 4:8-16 to discover what followed.
4. Cain murdered Abel out of jealousy. Describe God's total response to Cain in verses 13-15.

5. What can we learn about the dignity of life from God's response?

Read James 2:8-18.
6. Considering the origin of human persons, why is faith without

works dead (vv. 14-18)?

7. If life is sacred enough to warrant physical needs being met, as James suggests, how should you and I as individual Christians regard the life of a totalitarian head of state?

the life of a drug kingpin or a serial killer?

the lives of a minority (such as Whites in South Africa) that oppress a majority?

8. Applying James 2:9-17, which would be more deserving of a charitable contribution: the provision of basic needs assistance to a disabled veteran or to a single, unemployed mother of six children?

9. *Response:* Describe a biblical response to the examples of discrimination you gave in question 1. Be practical.

Study 3

Abortion

There is no doubt that a unique biological life exists in the fertilized ovum. Whether this life is potential life, rather than actual life—because it is not yet capable of independent existence outside the mother—is not a question that applies only to a fetus. For example, many people are alive only because of external aids such as a dialysis machine or a respirator.

Prolife advocates insist that the fertilized ovum is a life that should be protected and treated with dignity and respect, as a human life made in the image of God. Prochoice advocates believe that making abortion illegal does injustice to women by removing their right to have a safe abortion when, for a variety of reasons, the pregnancy is unwanted by the mother. They fear that a reversal of the 1973 *Roe* v. *Wade* decision, which made abortion legal, would lead to a proliferation of "back-alley" abortions and consequent increased suffering (and even death) of desperate women with little money and limited alternatives. These are complex questions which we must work through on the basis of Scripture.

Read Exodus 20:13.
1. Do you think the act of abortion differs from the act of murder? Why or why not?

Read Psalm 139; Jeremiah 1:4-5.
2. How do Jeremiah and the psalmist see themselves, as unborn children, from God's perspective?

Read Matthew 18:1-10.
3. What do you hear Jesus saying in Matthew 18 about the place of children in our lives and in the kingdom of heaven?

The following scenarios illustrate some of the common dilemmas that are faced by women and men as they contemplate abortion. Read them prayerfully, and in the light of Scripture.
Case 1: Mrs. Yentl is the carrier of a gene for a rare metabolic disease. At the twelfth week of pregnancy, an amniocentesis is performed; it shows that the fetus is undoubtedly affected. The prognosis is that the child is likely to have seizures, be mentally retarded

and suffer progressive failure to thrive in infancy. Mr. and Mrs. Yentl decide to have an abortion, as they wish to avoid the inevitable suffering that they and their child would experience if the child were allowed to be born.

Read 1 Corinthians 1:26-29.
4. Is mental retardation a justifiable reason for abortion?

Read Hebrews 4:15-16; Philippians 1:29.
5. How should we as Christians understand the issue of suffering posed by this family and the Scriptures?

Read Romans 5:3-5.
6. How could the birth of this child be a positive experience to a family like the Yentls?

Read Romans 15:1-2.
7. Should the Yentls reconsider their decision, what should the response of the community of believers be to the birth of this child?

What if you were their friends, and they decided to go through with the abortion?

Case 2: Dorothy Brown, an unmarried mother of two and a known abuser of alcohol and occasionally cocaine, is pregnant and seeks an abortion. The fetus is likely to grow poorly and to show signs of cocaine addiction at birth, with possible later mental retardation associated with fetal-alcohol-syndrome. This risk would be lessened if the mother could be admitted to a drug rehabilitation unit, but there are no such facilities available to pregnant women in this state.

8. Are the consequences of maternal substance abuse reasonable justification for aborting this fetus?

9. How does Miss Brown's situation differ from Mrs. Yentl's?

How does this affect your approach to her problem?

Read Luke 4:16-21 in which Jesus preaches his first sermon in the synagogue in Nazareth.

10. As followers of Jesus, how do we apply this teaching to people like Dorothy Brown?

11. In your opinion, are there any circumstances that justify the taking of fetal life?

How do you support your opinion in the light of Scripture?

12. *Response:* What practical alternatives can the church give to women who see abortion as their only hope?

For Further Study: Read 1 Peter 2:20; 3:14; Galatians 6:2; Romans 8:28 on suffering.

War

Christians *have tended to approach the subject of war from two* quite distinct positions. One side, held by nonviolent activists, says that war is unjustified in the light of the biblical teachings that all human life is sacred, made in the image of God, and that we are not to kill. The other position, called the "just war tradition," argues that war is acceptable under certain circumstances, such as in defense of human life or to ensure human rights and a just social order. The advocates of this position have established principles that should be satisfied before war is entered into and principles that should be adhered to during the conduct of a war. These principles are discussed at length in David Hollenbach's book *Nuclear Ethics* (see the resource section).

Jesus entered human history with a revolutionary statement: "Love your enemies and pray for those who persecute you, that you may be sons of your Father in heaven" (Mt 5:44-45).

1. Imagine that you are a Christian in Germany during the Holocaust. A Jewish couple comes to your house and asks you to hide them. Doing this would be breaking the law. What would you do?

Why?

Read Exodus 21:23-25; Matthew 5:38-48.
2. What changes do you see from the Old Testament to the New Testament regarding revenge?

3. What is Jesus saying to his disciples in Matthew about retribution for evil?

4. What new principle is Jesus laying down for his disciples?

Read Luke 6:27-38.

5. How does Jesus suggest that we treat our enemies?

6. Why are we to be given no credit for lending to those we know will repay us (v. 33)?

Read Joshua 1:1-5.

7. In Joshua 10 there is an account of a battle in which the Lord fought for Israel. In doing so, God was fulfilling promises he had given in Joshua 1, driving out the enemies of the Israelites so that his people could claim the Promised Land. Many people regard these accounts as justifying war against various groups viewed as our enemies. What do you think?

Read James 4:4-7.

8. What does the New Testament have to say about who our enemy is?

Read Ephesians 6:12-18.

9. What kind of warfare must Christians engage in on a daily basis?

10. How does the possession of eternal life influence our attitude to war, to the Holocaust, to the threat of nuclear war?

11. *Response:* Discuss how you can use the principles of Matthew 5:9, 44 to reflect the character of Christ in the world. What alternatives do we have to engaging in armed combat?

For Further Study: Compare Exodus 20:13 with Matthew 5:21-22. What does Jesus' response to Pilate at his trial (John 18:36) say about our allegiance to any constitutional authority?

Capital Punishment

The six o'clock news is on. A fire on Fifth Street has taken the lives of a mother and her four children. Police suspect the estranged husband and father of having started the fire. In another story, a masked man has brutally raped and killed a fourth victim. A jury has begun to deliberate the guilt or innocence of a woman charged with hiring a "hit man" to murder her husband.

Events like these have become commonplace in our world. Life has become very cheap. It has also become more difficult and stressful. Many are finding it hard to cope.

Several states have reinstituted the death penalty as a punishment and, many hope, a deterrent. A debate rages over the legitimacy of the state's right to take life even for heinous murders.

In the Christian community, opinion is divided as well. On the one hand are those who argue that it is the right of the state, under its divine mandate (Rom 13) to take life in meting out justice. They argue that the Christian is duty-bound to support the government in this discharge of its God-given mandate.

On another hand are Christians who hold that the government is not mandated to make laws that are contrary to God's moral law, which, under the dispensation of grace, seeks to redeem sinners. They argue that God reserves for himself the function of avenging the act of murder.

Each of us as followers of Jesus Christ and citizens of our country must develop a biblically based position on this sensitive question. To develop our position, we must search the Scriptures and pray for godly discernment.

1. How do you regard your government?

Read Romans 13:1-10.

2. Many argue that the instruction "Everyone must submit himself to the governing authorities" (v. 1) requires the Christian to support capital punishment when it is the law. Does the Christian have an alternative?

3. According to this passage, how is authority established (vv. 1-2)?

4. How is the person in authority described (vv. 3-7)?

5. According to this passage, what would the responsibilities of authorities be over human life?

6. From verses 8-10 do you think the government has to be just in order to exercise its authority?

7. What does this passage add to your understanding of God's expectations of both individuals and governments?

Read Exodus 21:12; Romans 3:21-31.
8. Exodus 21:12 requires people to be put to death if they kill another. How does Romans 3:21-31 turn this law upside down?

9. Verse 31 says that faith upholds the law. How does this passage uphold the law in Exodus?

10. Does a person forfeit his or her right to life when he or she takes the life of another?

11. *Response:* Does the practice of capital punishment diminish society's ability to regard life as sacred?

For Further Study: In what way and on what basis did Jesus depart from the law of Moses in John 7:23 and Matthew 19:8-9?

A Biblical View of Life

These studies have helped us to see several dimensions of human life from a biblical perspective. We have struggled with the application of biblical principles to real-life issues of war, abortion and capital punishment. Instead of finding clear-cut answers, we often end up having to make hard choices, weighing such things as the comparative worth of two lives, the lesser of two evils, the good of the individual versus the good of society, obedience to the law of the state or to the law of God.

As these choices face us on a day-to-day basis, we need to determine where we think our biblical faith would have us stand on these issues. Our final study addresses this goal.

1. Think of the last time you made a difficult ethical decision. What helped you to make your choice?

Read Matthew 5:1-26, 38-48.
2. This passage is Jesus' teaching to his disciples early in his ministry. What qualities does he identify in verses 1-12 as being worthy of blessing or happiness?

What are the rewards of these qualities?

3. How should these qualities be reflected in your response to a pregnant woman who had an illicit affair and now desires an abortion, as the child is not her husband's?

4. How does this passage call you to respond to a man who is imprisoned for brutally sodomizing and raping a nine-year-old girl?

5. How would these verses help you in responding to an action taken by the administration of your college or workplace that is clearly discriminatory against minorities? (You are a member of the majority group.)

6. How does this affect your reaction to a decision by Congress to fund a new anti-satellite missile?

7. What does it mean to be the salt of the earth and the light of the world (vv. 13-16)?

8. What is the consequence of our acting as salt and light in the world?

9. What does Jesus say about the necessity of Christians practicing and teaching the commandments (vv. 17-20)?

10. Jesus extends the commandment not to murder to include not holding anger toward others (vv. 22, 24-25). Can you think of any ways in which you as an individual, or we as a church, could address the prevention of killing, either one-on-one (murder) or nation-against-nation (war), by addressing the antecedent emotions and attitudes like anger?

11. How would this further fulfill the teachings of Jesus in verses 9 and 43-48?

12. *Response:* Pray that your faith in God will grow as you take a biblical stand on these issues, and that you will be prepared to suffer the cost of being God's representatives in the world.

Suggestions for Leaders

Leading a Bible discussion can be an enjoyable and rewarding experience. But it can also be intimidating—especially if you've never done it before. If this is how you feel, you're in good company. When God asked Moses to lead the Israelites out of Egypt, he replied, "O Lord, please send someone else to do it!" (Ex 4:13). But God's response to all of his servants—including you—is essentially the same: "My grace is sufficient for you" (2 Cor 12:9).

There is another reason you should feel encouraged. Leading a Bible discussion is not difficult if you follow certain guidelines. You don't need to be an expert on the Bible or a trained teacher. The suggestions listed below should enable you to effectively and enjoyably fulfill your role as leader.

Preparing for the Study

1. Ask God to help you understand and apply the passage in your own life. Unless this happens, you will not be prepared to lead others. Pray too for the various members of the group. Ask God to open your hearts to the message of his Word and motivate you to action.

2. Read the introduction to the entire guide to get an overview of the subject at hand and the issues which will be explored. If you want to do more reading on the topic, check out the resource section at the end of the guide for appropriate books and magazines.

3. As you begin each study, read and reread the assigned Bible passages to familiarize yourself with them. Read the passages suggested for further study as well. This will give you a broader picture of how these issues are discussed throughout Scripture.

4. This study guide is based on the New International Version of the Bible. It will help you and the group if you use this translation as the basis for your study and discussion.

5. Carefully work through each question in the study. Spend time in meditation and reflection as you consider how to respond.

6. Write your thoughts and responses in the space provided in the study guide. This will help you to express your understanding of the passage clearly.

7. It might help you to have a Bible dictionary handy. Use it to look up any unfamiliar words, names or places. (For additional help on how to study a passage, see chapter five of *Leading Bible Discussions,* IVP.)

8. Take the response portion of each study seriously. Consider what this means for your life—what changes you might need to make in your lifestyle and/or actions you need to take in the world. Remember that the group will follow your lead in responding to the studies.

Leading the Study

1. Begin the study on time. Open with prayer, asking God to help the group to understand and apply the passage.

2. Be sure that everyone in your group has a study guide. Encourage the group to prepare beforehand for each discussion by reading the introduction to the guide and by working through the questions in the study.

3. At the beginning of your first time together, explain that these studies are meant to be discussions, not lectures. Encourage the members of the group to participate. However, do not put pressure on those who may be hesitant to speak during the first few sessions.

4. Have a group member read the introductory paragraph at the beginning of the discussion. This will orient the group to the topic of the study.

5. Have a group member read aloud the passage to be studied. (When there is more than one passage, the Scripture is divided up throughout the study so that you won't have to keep several passages in mind at the same time.)

6. As you ask the questions, keep in mind that they are designed to be used just as they are written. You may simply read them aloud. Or you may prefer to express them in your own words. There may be times when it is appropriate to deviate from the study guide. For example, a question may have already been answered. If so, move on to the next question. Or someone may raise an important question not covered in the guide. Take time to discuss it, but try to keep the group from going off on tangents.

7. Avoid answering your own questions. If necessary, repeat or rephrase them until they are clearly understood. An eager group quickly becomes passive and silent if they think the leader will do most of the talking.

8. Don't be afraid of silence. People may need time to think about the question before formulating their answers.

9. Don't be content with just one answer. Ask, "What do the rest of you think?" or "Anything else?" until several people have given answers to the question.

10. Acknowledge all contributions. Try to be affirming whenever possible. Never reject an answer. If it is clearly off-base, ask, "Which verse led you to that conclusion?" or again, "What do the rest of you think?"

11. Don't expect every answer to be addressed to you, even though this will probably happen at first. As group members become more at ease, they will begin to truly interact with each other. This is one sign of healthy discussion.

12. Don't be afraid of controversy. It can be very stimulating. If you don't resolve an issue completely, don't be frustrated. Move on and keep it in mind for later. A subsequent study may solve the problem.

13. Periodically summarize what the group has said about the passage. This helps to draw together the various ideas mentioned and gives continuity to the study. But don't preach.

14. Don't skip over the response question. Be willing to get things started by describing how you have been convicted by the study and what action you'd like to take. Consider doing a service project as a group in response to what you're learning from the studies. Alternately, hold one another accountable to get involved in some kind of active service.

15. Conclude your time together with conversational prayer. Ask for God's help in following through on the commitments you've made.

16. End on time.

Many more suggestions and helps are found in *Small Group Leaders' Handbook* and *Good Things Come in Small Groups* (both from IVP). Reading through one of these books would be worth your time.

Resources

Publications

Hollenbach, David. *Nuclear Ethics: A Christian Moral Argument.* New York: Paulist Press, 1983.

Nelson, J. B., and Joanne Smith-Rohricht. "The Humanity in Abortion," in *Human Medicine: Ethical Perspectives on Today's Medical Issues.* Minneapolis: Augsburg, 1984.

Nelson, J. Robert. *Human Life.* Philadelphia: Fortress Press, 1984.

Six Steps for Non-Violent Social Change: Statement of Objectives and Purpose. Atlanta: Martin Luther King Center for Non-Violent Social Change, 1989.

United Methodist Council of Bishops. *In Defense of Creation: The Nuclear Crisis and a Just Peace.* Nashville: Graded Press, 1986.

World Christian magazine. P.O. Box 40010, Pasadena, Calif. 91104.

Organizations

Americans United for Life. 343 South Dearborn St., Suite 1804, Chicago, Ill. 60604.

Birthright. (800) 848-5683.

Conflict Resolution Division. The Carter Presidential Center, 1 Copenhill, Atlanta, Ga. 30307.

Feminists for Life. 811 E. 47th St., Kansas City, Mo. 64110; (816) 753-2130.

JustLife. Lancaster & City Aves., Philadelphia, Penn. 19151; (215) 645-9390.

Martin Luther King Center for Non-Violent Social Change, 449 Auburn Ave. N.E., Atlanta, Ga. 30312.

Sojourners, Box 29272, Washington, D.C. 20017.

SANCTITY OF LIFE

An unmarried, unemployed mother of two is pregnant. She abuses alcohol and occasionally cocaine. The fetus is likely to grow poorly, to show signs of cocaine addiction at birth, and to possibly experience mental retardation. How would you advise her? What biblical principles would you base your decision on?

Does being created in God's image suggest anything to us about capital punishment for murderers? What if the person in question is a serial killer? What about a drug kingpin?

In this guide E. Dawn Swaby-Ellis helps us explore what it means to talk about the "sanctity of life." In these six Bible studies she focuses particularly on the tough questions of abortion, war and capital punishment, guiding us to a biblical view of life.

E. Dawn Swaby-Ellis is assistant professor of pediatrics at Emory University in Atlanta. Prior to coming to the U.S., Dawn served on the faculty of the University of the West Indies in Kingston, Jamaica. She lives with her husband, Elward, and son, Jonathan, in the metropolitan Atlanta area.

GLOBAL ISSUES BIBLE STUDIES

from InterVarsity Press

Basic Human Needs by Bryan Truman
Economic Justice by Jana L. Webb
Environmental Stewardship by Ruth Goring Stewart
Fundamentalistic Religion by Eva and Joshi Jayaprakash
Healing for Broken People by Dan Harrison
Leadership in the 21st Century by Gordon Aeschliman

Multi-Ethnicity by Isaac Canales
People and Technology by Mary Fisher
Sanctity of Life by E. Dawn Swaby-Ellis
Spiritual Conflict by Arthur F. Glasser
Urbanization by Glandion Carney
Voiceless People by Chuck Shelton

ISBN 0-8308-4911-4

9 780830 849116